P-47
THUNDERBOLT
William N. Hess

Front cover illustration:
Thunderbolt of the 508th
Fighter Squadron, 404th
Fighter Group in flight at about
the end of the Second World
War. (L. Moon)

Back cover illustration:
Probably the last Thunderbolt
formation. These P-47s were
brought back from Peru in 1969
by Confederate Air Force. All
were flying by 1974 and this
formation was photographed on
25 February 1974. (CAF)

1. A forerunner of the P-47 was the XP-41. This aircraft was a high altitude design. It could exceed 300mph in level flight but was never put into production. (Fairchild Hiller)

P·47
THUNDERBOLT

William N. Hess

ARMS AND
ARMOUR

2. Alexander Kartveli, who designed the P-47. Contrary to popular designs of the day, he came up with a big airframe mated to a supercharged Pratt & Whitney R-2800 engine with great high-altitude potential. (Fairchild Hiller)

3. Test pilot L. L. Brabham took this XP-47B for its first test flight on 6 May 1941. Although it was lost on a later test flight, it was the first of many Thunderbolts to come down the line. (Fairchild Hiller)

INTRODUCTION

First published in Great Britain in
1989 by Arms and Armour Press,
Artillery House, Artillery Row,
London SW1P 1RT.

Distributed in the USA by Sterling
Publishing Co. Inc., 2 Park
Avenue, New York, NY 10016.

Distributed in Australia by
Capricorn Link (Australia) Pty.
Ltd., P.O. Box 665, Lane Cove,
New South Wales 2066, Australia.

British Library Cataloguing in
Publication Data:
Hess, William N.
P-47 Thunderbolt
1. Republic Aircraft P-47
aeroplanes
I. Title II. Series
623.74'64
ISBN 0-85368-927-X

Line illustrations courtesy of
Fairchild Hiller Republic Aviation
Division.

Designed and edited by DAG
Publications Ltd.
Designed by David Gibbons;
layout by Cilla Eurich; typeset by
Ronset Typesetters Ltd, Darwen,
Lancashire, and Typesetters
(Birmingham) Ltd, Warley, West
Midlands; camerawork by M&E
Reproductions, North Fambridge,
Essex; printed and bound in Great
Britain by The Alden Press,
Oxford.

Originally the Republic P-47 was to have been a conventional 1939 design, but only lightly armed with two machine-guns and powered by the new Allison V-1710 liquid-cooled engine, the lightweight aircraft would have been miserably obsolete before the prototype was finished.

Alexander Kartveli, the brilliant chief engineer of Republic, disagreed with the programme, and once war had erupted in Europe, he eagerly sought performance information from the combat area. Under his leadership Republic completely redesigned its aircraft and produced one of the outstanding fighters of the Second World War. The new XP-47B was a heavyweight built around the Pratt & Whitney R-2800 engine which developed 2,000 horsepower. A turbo-supercharger made it a high-altitude performer and the light armament was replaced by four .50 machine-guns in each wing.

The heavy fighter was not an instant winner with the pilots that initially took it to combat. The American ex-Eagle Squadron pilots hated it from the beginning, but the 56th Fighter Group pilots who initially trained on the P-47 loved it. Low-altitude air to air combat remained a problem until a paddle blade propeller was added, but high-altitude combat was a different story.

Its short range was a distinct handicap until the auxiliary fuel tank problems had been resolved, but when it came to strafing and dive-bombing the big P-47 excelled. Following D-Day in France, the Thunderbolts performed magnificently in ground support until the end of the war.

A late arrival in the Far East and the Pacific, the P-47 did a fine job in the ground support role in Burma and China. In the South and Central Pacific it served in small numbers until late in the war, but wherever it served it turned in a brilliant performance marked by the great destruction of which it was capable. Despite its great capability, however, the P-47 was soon scrapped after the war. Who was to know that as early as 1950 its ground-support performance would have been a real blessing in Korea.

Today very few Thunderbolts survive. Yet the old P-47, T-Bolt, Thunderbolt or Jug, whatever you care to call it, left many fond memories with the men it carried to victory and to the many 'dog faces' down in the mud whose lives it saved.

▲4

▲5

4. This was the first fully completed XP-47B, resplendent in olive drab warpaint. (Fairchild Hiller)

5. This P-47D-20 was the first model to be fitted with belly shackles and wing tank adaptors. It also incorporated the paddle blade propeller to improve low altitude and climbing performance. (Fairchild Hiller)

6. Republic built only two TP-47Gs which were two-seater aircraft. It was designed for use in teaching combat tactics and evasive manoeuvres. (Fairchild Hiller)

7. High-altitude combat presented many problems. In the endeavour to solve these the XP-47E, which incorporated a pressurized cabin, was built. Although a one-off the aircraft provided much vital research information for future designs. (Fairchild Hiller)

8. One of the early P-47s assigned to the Eighth Air Force in England. Aircraft were painted olive drab overall on upper surfaces and neutral grey underneath. Note yellow circle outlining national insignia on fuselage. (USAF)

9. First to fly the P-47 in combat was the 4th Fighter Group. This unit was composed of former Spitfire pilots from the American Eagle Squadrons of the Royal Air Force. They said it was like 'giving up a thoroughbred horse for a plough horse'. (USAF)

10. Thunderbolt of the 83rd Fighter Squadron, 78th Fighter Group. White nose and white stripes on tail were for fast recognition purposes. (M. Havelaar)

▲8   ▼9

▼10

11. A line-up of Thunderbolts from the 63rd Fighter Squadron of the 56th Fighter Group. The 56th received the first P-47s off the assembly line, trained in them and swore by them. (USAF)

12. P-47 of the 4th Fighter Group, fitted with a 75-gallon drop tank. The Thunderbolts were handicapped for escort duty by their lack of range. (USAF)

13. Captain Charles P. London of the 78th Fighter Group, here being decorated by RAF Air Marshall Sir Leigh-Mallory, became the first Eighth Air Force ace when he downed his fourth and fifth enemy aircraft on 30 July 1943. (USAF)

14. Thunderbolts of the 83rd Fighter Squadron, 78th Fighter Group ready for take-off. They are fitted with 108-gallon paper drop tanks which increased their range to 325 miles. (USAF)

15. P-47s were rugged aircraft. This 56th Fighter Group aircraft took a beating from German 20mm cannon and made it home. (USAF)

16. 'Zombie' from the 361st Fighter Squadron, 356th Fighter Group following a wheels-up landing. These were often caused by battle damage to the hydraulic system. Other than damage to the propeller, 'sudden stoppage' of the engine and sheet metal damage this Thunderbolt seems none the worse for wear. (AF Museum)

▲13   ▼14

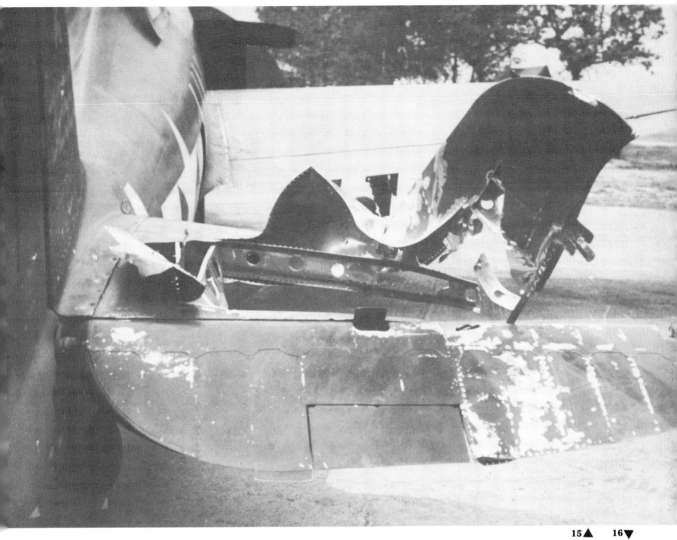

19. Thunderbolts of the 78th Fighter Group lined up at their base at Duxford. All the 'MX' marked aircraft belong to the 82nd Fighter Squadron. The 'CV' Thunderbolt is a visitor from the 368th Fighter Squadron of the 359th Fighter Group. (USAF)

20. On a mission to Bremen on 26 November 1943, these pilots of the 56th Fighter Group downed 26 enemy aircraft. Pilots in this famous photograph are (left to right): Captain W. V. Cook; Lieutenants S. B. Morrill, J. B. Bryant, J. H. Truluck; Captain Walker Mahurin; Lieutenant Harold Comstock; Lieutenant Colonel Dave Schilling; Majors F. S. Gabreski, J. C. Stewart; Lieutenants F. W. Klibbe, J. D. Brown, Eugene O'Neill, Raymond Petty, I. F. Valento and A. Carcione. (USAF)

▲17

▼18

17. Colonel Hubert 'Hub' Zemke, famed leader of the 56th Fighter Group which became known as 'Zemke's Wolfpack'. The 56th was the only Eighth Air Force Group to retain P-47s up to the end of the war in Europe. (USAF)

18. Major Walter Beckham was the leading Eighth Air Force ace with eighteen aerial victories scored flying the P-47 before he was shot down while strafing. (W. Beckham)

▲21 ▼22

21. Captain Robert S. Johnson of the 56th Fighter Group after he had downed Nos. 26 and 27 victories on 8 May 1944. Johnson was the first to surpass the 26 aerial victory record of America's First World War ace, Captain Eddie Rickenbacker. (R. S. Johnson)

22. Another example of nose art is this P-47 of Lieutenant Chester V. Harker of the 486th Fighter Squadron, 352nd Fighter Group. Note gloves and goggles worn by pilot. Hand and face coverage were essential in case of fire in the cockpit. (via T. Ivie)

23. The invasion of the Continent brought about the black-and-white invasion stripes for aircraft identity over the beaches. This 78th Fighter Group P-47D-28 is also fitted with a bubble canopy which greatly enhanced visibility. (USAF)

24. Armourers loading .50 calibre ammunition in the wing boxes. The eight guns of the Thunderbolt packed a punch that spelled immediate and heavy damage to their targets, both in the air and on the ground. (USAF)

25. By D-Day many of the aircraft of the Eighth Air Force had given up their olive drab paint and were flying in natural motif. This P-47, belonging to the 84th Fighter Squadron, is resplendent in group black-and-white checkered nose denoting the 78th Fighter Group plus black-and-white invasion stripes for D-Day and subsequent identification. (M. Havelaar)

23▲   24▼

25▼

▲26

▲27

▼28

26. Thunderbolts of the 56th Fighter Group lined up for take-off carrying 150-gallon flat metal fuel tanks. These tanks gave the P-47 a range of 375 miles and were used up to the end of the war. (USAF)

27. Captain Michael Gladych, Polish ace who flew P-47s with the 56th Fighter Group, is shown here with his aircraft 'Pengie III' and his ground crew. Gladych downed ten enemy aircraft with the Eighth Air Force after being credited with 8½ victories with the RAF. (USAF)

28. Lieutenant Colonel F. S. Gabreski, top P-47 ace, with 28 aerial victories plus another on the ground. Gabreski flew with the 56th Fighter Group until he went down while strafing on 20 July 1944. He was taken prisoner and spent the rest of the war in Stalag Luft I at Barth in Germany. (USAF)

29. A mixed formation of Thunderbolts from the 63rd Fighter Squadron. The removal of the invasion stripes from the wings of the aircraft dates this photograph after September 1944. Note that some aircraft are in olive drab while others are natural metal. Even one old razorback P-47 is in the formation. (USAF)

30. Mechanics of the 56th Fighter Group converted this 'war weary', hence Category 'E', to a two-seater. Note the long cockpit area and the elongated hatch. (via Stafford)

▲31　▼32

31. Instead of converting to P-51s, the 56th Fighter Group received the only P-47Ms in January 1945. The new engine was capable of a top speed of 473mph at 32,000 feet. However, constant engine troubles made the aircraft ineffective until April 1945. (USAF)

32. Overhead view of the P-47 cockpit. The windshield was very thick bullet-proof glass, but the plexiglass canopy was much thinner and vulnerable to all shorts of shot and shell. (USAF)

33. Thunderbolts of the Ninth Tactical Air Force were based in England before D-Day. Here two P-47s of the 373rd Fighter Group head out on a mission. (USAF)

▼33

34. Primary duty of the Ninth Air Force was dive-bombing and strafing. Here Thunderbolts of the 36th Fighter Group taxi out laden with 500lb bombs and auxiliary fuel tanks. (C. R. Queen)

35. 'Chunky', a Ninth Air Force Thunderbolt has propeller pulled through by ground crew before pre-flight. The aircraft has brand-new black-and-white ID stripes painted on wings and fuselage. (USAF)

36. As soon as Air Force engineers could clear strips in Normandy the pilots were using them. Here planes of the 405th Fighter Group are being serviced on such a field. (USAF)

▲37 ▼38 ▼39

37. Pierced steel planking was in great demand for runways, taxiways and hardstands in France. Here Thunderbolts ready themselves for take-off from a PSP strip. (USAF)

38. Bomb-laden P-47s of the 390th Fighter Squadron, 366th Fighter Group taxi down snow-lined strip at Belgian base Y-29 en route to runway. Regardless of weather, Ninth Air Force Thunderbolts flew many missions during the Battle of the Bulge in December 1944. (P. Ollerton)

39. Excellent close-up of a P-47 in Normandy loaded with auxillary gas tanks filled with napalm. This highly combustible jellied gasoline was one of the most lethal weapons introduced into tactical airpower. (C. R. Queen)

40. 'The Eyes of Texas' comes in for a landing. This 411th Fighter Squadron Thunderbolt was probably based at Y-10 in Belgium when this was taken. (T. Ambrose)

41. P-47 with a Malcolm hood, 'B' Cominbac of the 412th Fighter Squadron, 373rd Fighter Group on hardstand in Belgium. Note drop tanks and dolly sitting in mud alongside. Bombs are loaded for the next mission. (T. Ambrose)

42. 'My Mozelle' of the 508th Fighter Squadron, 404th Fighter Group at A-92, St. Trond, Belgium. Well over 100 bombing mission symbols are painted just aft of cowling. (L. Moon)

43. This photograph typifies the field operations of IX, XIX, and XXIX TACs which were under Ninth Air Force. Here is a P-47 on a grassy strip, 500lb bomb on loading dolly, ammunition cans and boxes scattered around. Tents in background. (T. Ambrose)

▲40 ▼41

42▲　43▼

P-47D THUNDERBOLT

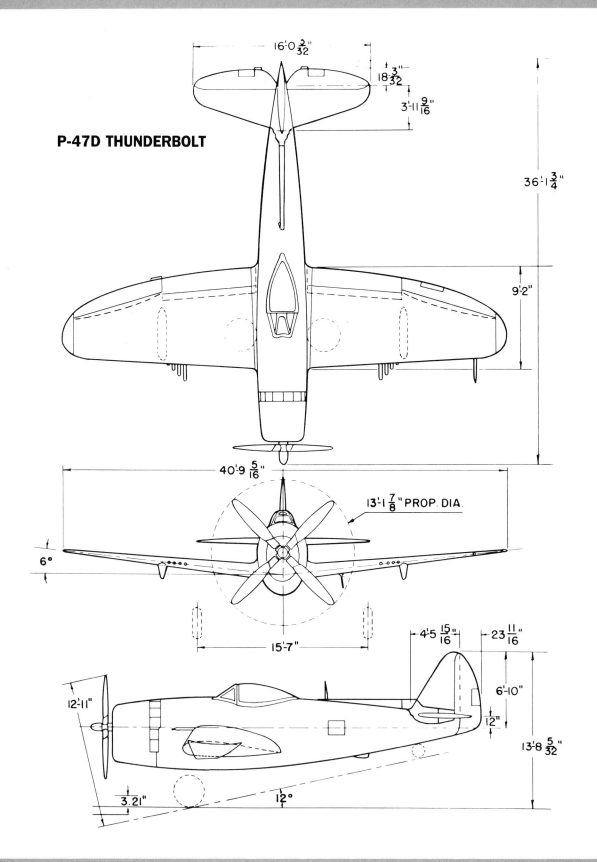

16'-0 2/32"

18' 3/32"

3'-11 9/16"

36'-1 3/4"

9'-2"

40'-9 5/16"

13'-1 7/8" PROP. DIA.

6°

15'-7"

4'-5 15/16"

23 11/16"

6'-10"

12"

13'-8 5/32"

12'-11"

3.21"

12°

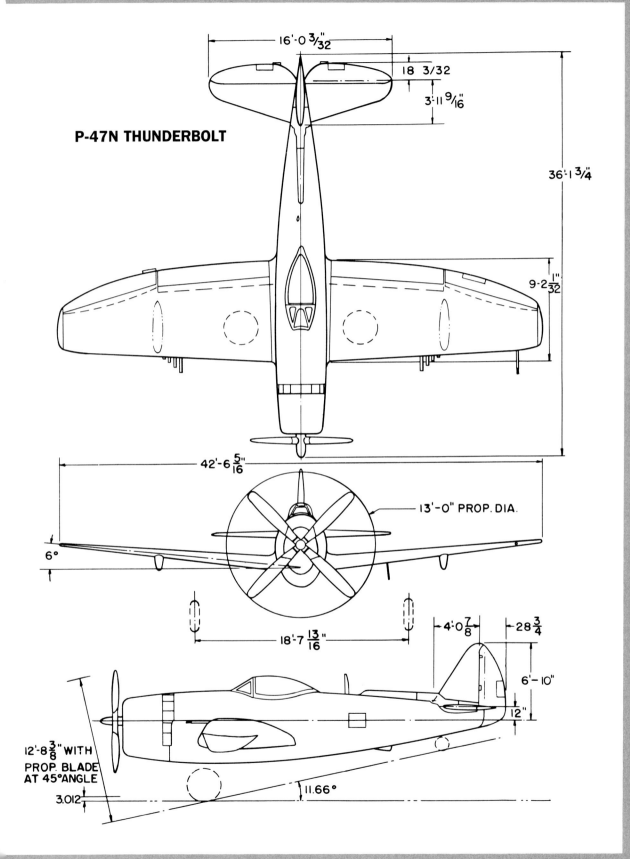

P-47N THUNDERBOLT

SPECIFICATIONS

Model	Wingspan	Length	Height	Weight (empty)	Take-off Weight (Max.)	Power Plant	Range (miles)	Max Speed (mph)	Max. Ceiling	Armament	No. Built	First Flight
XP-47B	40ft 9¾in	35ft	12ft 8in	9,189lb	12,700lb	XR-2800-17 2,000hp	575	412	38,000ft	Eight .50	(1)	6 May 41
P-47B	40ft 9¾in	35ft 3¼in	12ft 8in	9,346lb	13,360lb	R-2800-21 2,000hp	550	340	42,000ft	Eight .50	171	18 Mar. 42*
P-47C	40ft 9¾in	36ft 1¾in	14ft 1¾in	10,000lb	14,925lb	R-2800-21 2,000hp	640	353	42,000ft	Eight .50	602	14 Sept. 42*
P-47D	40ft 9¾in	36ft 1¾in	14ft 7in	10,000lb	19,400lb	R-2800-63 2,000hp	475	356	42,000ft	Eight .50	12,602	
XP-47H	40ft 9¾in	38ft 4in	14ft 2in	11,442lb	15,135lb	Chrysler XIV-220-1	770	414	36,000ft	Six .50	(2)	26 July 45
XP-47J	41ft	33ft 3in	14ft 2in	9,835lb	15,135lb	R-2800-57 2,300hp	765	507	45,000ft	Six .50	1	26 Nov. 43
P-47M	40ft 9¾in	36ft 4in	14ft 9in	10,423lb	15,500lb	R-2800-57 2,800hp	530	400	41,000ft	Eight .50	130	Dec. 1944*
P-47N	42ft 7in	36ft 1in	14ft 8in	11,000lb	20,700lb	R-2800-57-73-77 2,800hp	800	397	43,000ft	Eight .50	1,816	Sept. 1944

*First delivery.

SQUADRON LETTERS

Sqn	Letters	Sqn	Letters	Sqn	Letters	Sqn	Letters
Eighth Air Force		374	B7	388	C4	Royal Air Force	
334	QP	375	E2	389	A6	5	OQ
335	WD	376	E9	390	B2	30	RS
336	VF			391	A8	34	EG
61	HV	Ninth Air Force		392	H5	42	AW
62	LM	22	3T	393	8L	60	MU
63	UN	23	7U	394	4N	79	NV
82	MX	53	6V	395	9D	81	FL
83	HL	492	F4	396	C2	113	AD
84	WZ	493	I7	397	D3	123	XE
328	PE	494	6M	404	9Q	131	NX
486	PZ	10	T5	405	8N	134	GQ
487	HO	81	2N	406	4W	135	WK
350	LH	313	W3	410	R3	146	WA
351	YJ	353	FT	411	U9	258	ZT
352	SX	355	GQ	412	V5	261	FJ
354	WR	356	AJ	506	4K	615	KW
357	OS	365	CH	507	Y8		
358	YF	366	IA	508	7J		
359	OC	367	CP	509	G9		
360	PI	377	E4	510	2Z		
361	QI	378	G8	511	K4		
368	CV	379	B8	512	L3		
369	IV	386	D5	513	4P		
370	CS	387	B4	514	O7		

CAMOUFLAGE AND MARKINGS

European Theatre of Operations: P-47s assigned to Eighth Air Force had upper surfaces of wings, tail and fuselage painted matt Dark Olive Drab; the lower surfaces were sprayed with Neutral Grey. The groups were assigned call letters, which were painted on the fuselage in white. In February 1943 the Eighth Air Force P-47s were painted with white identification markings on the cowling and across vertical and horizontal tail surfaces; this was to avoid mistaking the Thunderbolt for the Focke Wulf 190.

Individual group markings were initiated in February 1944 by the 56th Fighter Group. In March 1944 all Eighth Air Force groups began their adoption of the colourful individual group markings.

In spring 1944 P-47s began to arrive still in their natural silver finish. Late in the war the 56th Fighter Group began to use some experimental camouflage schemes, Dark Green and Ocean Grey and various shades of two-tone grey.

Mediterranean Theatre of Operations: Basic paint schemes were the same as those in the Eighth Air Force. They also adopted individual group markings and primarily utilized individual aircraft numbers rather than squadron letters.

Pacific Theatre of Operations: Originally Olive Drab and Neutral Grey. White tails and wing leading edges were utilized for identification purposes.

Royal Air Force in Burma: Temperate Land Scheme of Dark Green and Dark Earth on upper surfaces and Medium Sea Grey under surfaces.

DEPLOYMENT

Group	Squadrons	Period

EUROPEAN THEATRE OF OPERATIONS

Eighth Air Force

Group	Squadrons	Period
4	334, 335, 336	Feb. 43 – Feb. 44
56	61, 62, 63	Feb. 43 – Oct. 45
78	82, 83, 84	Feb. 43 – Dec. 44
352	328, 486, 487	July 43 – April 44
353	350, 351, 352	July 43 – Oct. 44
355	354, 357, 358	July 43 – April 44
356	359, 360, 361	Aug. 43 – Nov. 44
359	368, 369, 370	Nov. 43 – May 44
361	374, 375, 376	Dec. 43 – May 44

Ninth Air Force

Group	Squadrons	Period
36	22, 23, 53	April 44 – Feb. 46
48	492, 493, 494	March 44 – Aug. 45
50*	10, 81, 313	March 44 – Aug. 45
354	353, 355, 356	Nov. 44 – Feb. 45
358*	365, 366, 367	Oct. 43 – July 45
362	377, 378, 379	Dec. 43 – Aug. 45
365	386, 387, 388	Dec. 43 – Sept. 45
366	389, 390, 391	Jan. 44 – Aug. 46
367	392, 393, 394	Feb. 45 – July 45
368	395, 396, 397	Feb. 44 – Aug. 46
371**	404, 405, 406	March 44 – Oct. 45
373	410, 411, 412	April 44 – July 45
404	506, 507, 508	April 44 – Aug. 45
405	509, 510, 511	March 44 – July 45
406	512, 513, 514	April 44 – Aug. 46

33 FS Iceland operational in P-47s April 44 – May 45.

MEDITERRANEAN THEATRE OF OPERATIONS

Group	Squadrons	Period
27	522, 523, 524	June 44 – Oct. 45
57	64, 65, 66	Jan. 44 – Aug. 45
79	85, 86, 87	March 44 – June 47
86	525, 526, 527	June 44 – March 46
324	314, 315, 316	July 44 – Oct. 45
325	317, 318, 319	Nov. 43 – May 44
332	99, 100, 301, 302	April 44 – June 44
350	345, 346, 347	July 44 – July 45

Brazilian Air Force
1 Grupo de Caca attached to 350 FG, US Fifth Air Force, MTO
Oct. 44 – June 45

PACIFIC THEATRE OF OPERATIONS

Fifth Air Force

Group	Squadrons	Period
8	36	Dec. 43 – Feb. 44
35	39, 40, 41	Dec. 43 – March 45
49	9	Nov. 43 – April 44
58	69, 310, 311	Feb. 44 – Dec. 45
348	340, 341, 342	June 43 – March 45
348	460	Sept. 44 – March 45

*To 1st TAF Nov. 44. **1st TAF Nov. 44 – Feb. 45.

Mexican Air Force
201 Escuadron Aeroeo de Pelea attached to 58 FG,
US Fifth Air Force May 45 – Oct. 45

Seventh Air Force

Group	Squadrons	Period
318	19, 73, 333	June 44 – Dec. 45
413	1, 21, 34	May 45 – Oct. 46
414	413, 437, 456	July 44 – Sept. 46
507	463, 464, 465	June 45 – May 46

CHINA, BURMA AND INDIA

Group	Squadrons	Period
1 Air Commando	5 C, 6 C	Sept. 44 – May 45
33	58, 59, 60	April 44 – Oct. 45
80	88, 89, 90	May 44 – Oct. 45
81	91, 92, 93	April 44 – Dec. 45

ROYAL AIR FORCE

Group	Squadrons	Period
	5	Sept. 44 – March 46
	30	July 44 – Dec. 45
	34	March 45 – Oct. 45
	42	June 45 – Dec. 45
	60	June 45 – Oct. 46
	79	July 44 – Dec. 45
	81	June 45 – June 46
	113	April 45 – Oct. 45
	123 (became 81)	Sept. 44 – June 45
	131	June 45 – Dec. 45
	134 (became 131)	Sept. 44 – June 45
	135 (became 615)	June 44 – April 45
	146 (became 42)	June 44 – June 45
	258	Sept. 44 – Dec. 45
	261	July 44 – Sept. 45
	615	June 45 – Sept. 45

FRENCH AIR FORCE

Group	Squadrons	Period
II/5	4	March 44 – July 47
II/3	4	May 44 – July 47
I/4	3, 4	July 44 – July 47
I/5	3	Sept. 44 – July 47
III/3	4	Oct. 44 – March 46
III/6	3	Feb. 45 – March 46

MODEL KITS CURRENTLY AVAILABLE

Scale	Manufacturer	Model
1/32	Revell	P-47D Bubbletop
1/32	Revell	P-47D Razorback
1/48	Monogram	P-47D Razorback
1/48	Monogram	P-47D Bubbletop
1/48	Testors	P-47D Razorback/Bubbletop
1/48	Arii	Razorback
1/72	Hasegawa	Razorback
1/72	Hasegawa	Bubbletop
1/72	Heller	P-47N
1/72	Matchbox	P-47D Razorback

44. Crew chief rides wing on taxi-out of 365th Fighter Group P-47. Ground crewman often did this to help keep the pilot on narrow taxi strips laid on mud, and to guide pilots in dusty conditions. (USAF)

45. This P-47, recovered after being downed by the Germans, was liberated in Luftwaffe markings at an airbase near Gottingen, Germany. (USAF)

46. 'Martha' was a P-47D used for training at Myrtle Beach, South Carolina, by the 404th Fighter Group before their departure for Europe. (L. Moon)

47. P-47 in foreground is 'Hollywood Highhatter' flown by Captain Paul Conger of the 56th Fighter Group. (W. Hess)

48. Razorback P-47 of the 56th Fighter Group fitted with 150-gallon drop tank. Note high gloss of aircraft from waxing. (W. Hess)

▲49

49. 'Pittsburg Pattie', personal mount of Lieutenant George Novotny, 8-victory ace of the 325th Fighter Group, Fifteenth Air Force in Italy. (G. Novotny)

50. P-47D 'Mary' flew in Italy with the 27th Fighter Group, Twelfth Air Force, whose P-47s

▼50

did yeoman duty supporting the advancing Fifth Army. (USAF)

51. P-47 of the 373rd Fighter Group, Ninth Air Force on a grass strip in France. By late summer of 1944 most razorbacks and olive drab paint jobs were gone. (T. Ambrose)

52. Lieutenant D. McDonald of the 325th Fighter Group flew No. 42. Note the stripes on the cowling and canopy outline. (via E. McDowell)

53. Formation of P-47s from the 325th Fighter Group. The numerals on the fuselage

denoted not only individual but also squadron numbers. These numbers indicate the 319th Fighter Squaron which used the 70-99 numerical sequence. (via E. McDowell)

51▲ 52▼

53▼

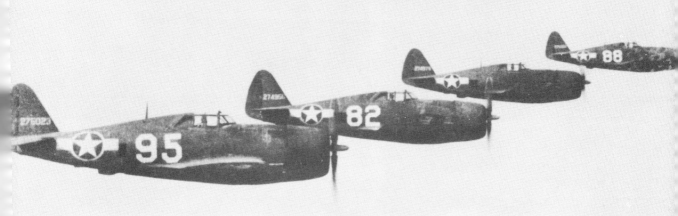

54. Top Thunderbolt ace in the Fifteenth Air Force was Major H. H. Green of the 325th Fighter Group who scored ten of his eighteen victories flying P-47s. Green destroyed four Ju 52s, a Dornier 217 and a MC 202 on a mission to Udine on 30 January 1944. (H. Green)

55. These silver razorback P-47s are units of the 79th Fighter Group. Flying from bases in Italy they provided close support for ground forces and won a Distinguished Unit Citation for low-altitude support at the River Santero, 16–20 April 1945. (USAF)

56. P-47s of the 347th Fighter Squadron, 350th Fighter Group on hardstand at base outside Pisa. The 350th destroyed many bridges and neutralized airfields in northern Italy. (USAF)

57. This Thunderbolt from the 350th Fighter Group was hit by flak on 12 January 1945, near Lake Garda, Italy and made it home. The pilot, Lieutenant Edwin L. King, surveys his oil covered aircraft. (F. Smith)

▲54

▲55

▲58 ▼59

58. P-47 of the 1st Air Commando Group based in India. This aircraft is fitted with long-range auxiliary fuel tanks. Note radio compass ring behind cockpit. (USAF)

59. Aircraft of the 91st Fighter Squadron, 81st Fighter Group lined up at a Chinese airbase. This unit supported Chinese ground troops. (USAF)

60. 'My Jewel' from the 81st Fighter Group is fitted with 75-gallon auxiliary fuel tanks and the bomb racks are loaded with what appears to be fragmentation bombs. (USAF)

61. 'Oh! Pudgy' belonged to the 348th Fighter Group, Fifth Air Force. The 348th was the initial Thunderbolt unit assigned to the SW Pacific. Note white tail surfaces and wing leading edges fore ID purposes. (USAF)

62. This colourful Thunderbolt was the personal aircraft of Lieutenant Marvin Grant, 7-victory ace of the 348th Fighter Group. (M. Grant)

▼60

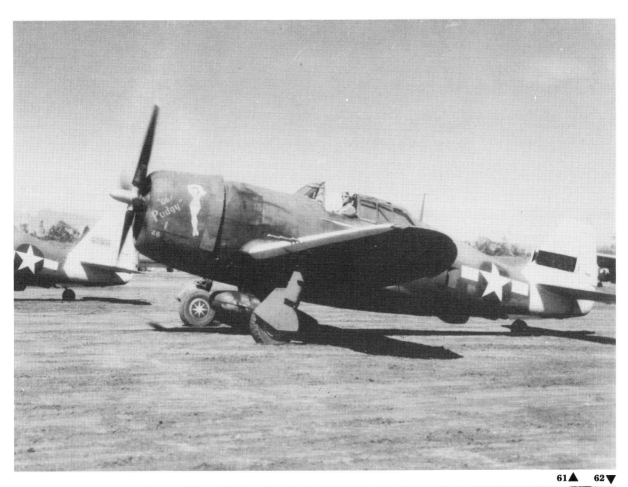

▲63　▼64

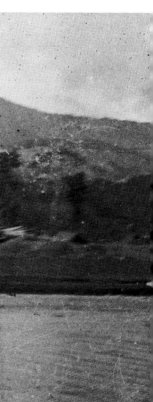

63. Major D. 'Bill' Dunham, 16-victory ace of the 348th Fighter Group, and his crew chief. Note two ships also symbolized as destroyed. (W. Dunham)

64. Colourful overhead photograph emphasizing white tail section against OD paint scheme of the 348th Fighter Group. (USAF)

65. Top-scoring Thunderbolt ace in the Pacific was Colonel Neale Kearby, Commanding Officer and 22-victory scorer of the 348th Fighter Group. Kearby won the Medal of Honor for the destruction of six Japanese fighters in one combat on 11 October 1943. (USAF)

66. 'Darling Dottie' flown by Captain John T. Moore of the 341st Fighter Squadron was painted in a most unusual OD and natural metal scheme. (T. K. Lewis)

65 ▲   66 ▼

67. Airborne! This 318th Fighter Group P-47 rises from the deck of the USS *Manilla Bay.* The group was transported from their base in Hawaii to the South Pacific in the carrier. (USAF)

68. This Saipan-based Thunderbolt is fitted with 500lb bombs and an auxiliary tank loaded with napalm. The 318th Fighter Group pilots flew all day and were harassed by enemy snipers at night. (USAF)

69. The P-47Ns of the 507th Fighter Group began combat operations from Ie Shima in July 1945. The P-47N was capable of very long-range missions with internal wing tanks and auxiliary drop tanks. (R. Forest)

70. This P-47N parked on a coral hardstand belonged to the 28th Fighter Squadron of the 413th Fighter Group. Coral on the Pacific islands, when crushed and packed down, made excellent paving for airfields. (D. Schlueter)

▲67　▼68

71. The insignia on Major Byrne's Thunderbolt exemplifies the task of taking off fully loaded from Ie Shima. The runway had a high cliff at each end. A number of P-47s failed to gain flying speed and crashed off the end of the runway. (D Schlueter)

72. Thunderbolt Is of 30 Squadron, RAF, taxi past the Hawker Hurricanes they replaced in Burma. (IWM)

73. The Thunderbolts of No. 5 Squadron, RAF, taxi out for another ground-support mission over Burma. The dark, two-tone, olive drab jungle paint scheme was standard in late 1944. (via R. C. Jones)

74. Take-off of an RAF Thunderbolt from 73 OTU Fayid in Egypt. Many of the RAF pilots who went to Burma received their conversion training at Fayid. (via R. T. Jones)

75. P-47D assigned to GC III/6 of the Free French Air Force. A number of French Thunderbolt squadrons flew with the First Tactical Air Force supporting ground forces in France. (via J. Cuny)

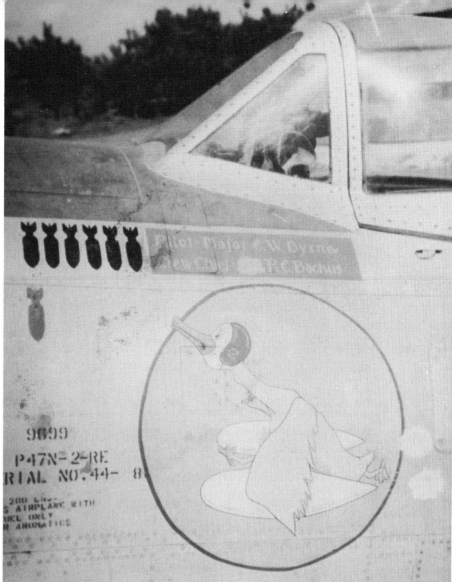

▲71   ▼72

73▲ 74▼

75▼

▲76

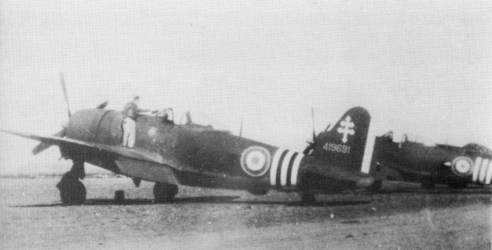

▲77

76. Crew chiefs guide P-47s of the Free French Air Force along a snow-covered airfield in the winter of 1944. Note 500lb bombs slung under each wing. (IWM)

77. Thunderbolts from GC III/3 'Ardennes' Free French Air Force. Note Cross of Lorraine insignia on tail and invasion stripes on fuselage. (via J. Cuny)

78. The Republic XP-47H was built to test the Chrysler XIV-2220-1 16-cylinder inverted vee engine. The test model reached a top speed of 490mph, but only two were built. (Fairchild Hiller)

79. The first conventional aircraft to exceed 500mph in level flight was the Republic P-47J. This model was lighter than the production P-47s and used a CH-5 turbo-supercharger. (Fairchild Hiller)

▲80

80. The Republic XP-72 was built around the Pratt & Whitney R-4360 engine which, at 3450hp, was the most powerful piston engine developed during the Second World War. Only two were built due to the rapid development of

jet aircraft in 1944. (Fairchild Hiller)

81. This pilot from the 512th Fighter Squadron of the 406th Fighter Group flies with canopy open and takes in the sights of occupied Germany. This

squadron, too, has adopted fancy paint schemes on their aircraft. (B. Kruase)

82. A brilliantly marked P-47D flown by Colonel Robert L. Baseler upon his return to the United States. 'Big Stud' was

also the name of his aircraft when he commanded the 'Checkertail Clan' 325th Fighter Group in Italy. (R. Baseler)

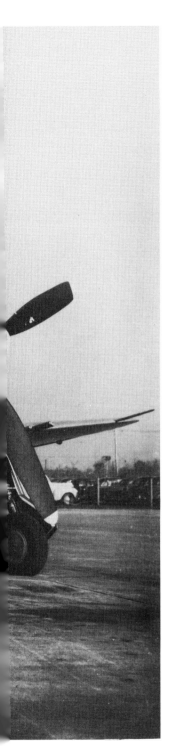

81▲   82▼

▲83

▲84

83. These P-47Ns belonged to the Hawaii Air National Guard in 1946. Although used by some Air National Guard units, the number was not large nor were the P-47s used long after the war. (Cassidy)

84. 'Undilla Killa' was one of the Peruvian Thunderbolts restored by Confederate Air Force of Harlingen, Texas, in 1973. The markings were those of Lieutenant Russell Kline who flew with the 355th Fighter Squadron during the war. (G. Bavousett)

85. The Puerto Rican Air National Guard reworked this P-47N and flew it on several tours around the United Sates in the early 1970s. (USAF)

86. 'Little Demon', beautifully restored razorback P-47, is one of the very few Thunderbolts flying today. The aircraft, which is finished in the markings of Eighth Air Force ace, Major Walter Beckham, now belongs to the Lone Star Air Museum in Galveston, Texas. (W. Hess)

...tofax series

...ictorial studies of military subjects for the
...orian and enthusiast. Each title features a carefully-
...set of photographs plus a data section of facts and figures
...he topic covered. With line drawings and detailed captioning,
every volume represents a succinct and valuable study of the
subject. New and forthcoming titles:

Warbirds
F-111 Aardvark
P-47 Thunderbolt
B-52 Stratofortress
Stuka!
Jaguar
US Strategic Air Power:
  Europe 1942–1945
Dornier Bombers
RAF in Germany

Vintage Aircraft
German Naval Air Service
Sopwith Camel
Fleet Air Arm, 1920–1939
German Bombers of WWI

Soldiers
World War One: 1914
World War One: 1915
World War One: 1916
Union Forces of the American
  Civil War
Confederate Forces of the
  American Civil War
Luftwaffe Uniforms
British Battledress 1945–1967
  (2 vols)

Warships
Japanese Battleships, 1897–
  1945
Escort Carriers of World War
  Two
German Battleships, 1897–
  1945
Soviet Navy at War, 1941–1945
US Navy in World War Two,
  1943–1944
US Navy, 1946–1980 (2 vols)
British Submarines of World
  War One

Military Vehicles
The Chieftain Tank
Soviet Mechanized Firepower
  Today
British Armoured Cars since
  1945
NATO Armoured Fighting
  Vehicles
The Road to Berlin
NATO Support Vehicles

The *Illustrated* series

The internationally successful range of photo albums devoted to
current, recent and historic topics, compiled by leading authors
and representing the best means of obtaining your own photo
archive.

Warbirds
US Spyplanes
USAF Today
Strategic Bombers, 1945–1985
Air War over Germany
Mirage
US Naval and Marine Aircraft
  Today
USAAF in World War Two
B-17 Flying Fortress
Tornado
Junkers Bombers of World War
  Two
Argentine Air Forces in the
  Falklands Conflict
F-4 Phantom Vol II
Army Gunships in Vietnam
Soviet Air Power Today
F-105 Thunderchief
Fifty Classic Warbirds
Canberra and B-57
German Jets of World War Two

Vintage Warbirds
The Royal Flying Corps in
  World War One
German Army Air Service in
  World War One
RAF between the Wars
The Bristol Fighter
Fokker Fighters of World War
  One
Air War over Britain, 1914–
  1918
Nieuport Aircraft of World War
  One

Tanks
Israeli Tanks and Combat
  Vehicles
Operation Barbarossa
Afrika Korps
Self-Propelled Howitzers
British Army Combat Vehicles
  1945 to the Present
The Churchill Tank
US Mechanized Firepower
  Today
Hitler's Panzers
Panzer Armee Afrika
US Marine Tanks in World War
  Two

Warships
The Royal Navy in 1980s
The US Navy Today
NATO Navies of the 1980s
British Destroyers in World
  War Two
Nuclear Powered Submarines
Soviet Navy Today
British Destroyers in World
  War One
The World's Aircraft Carriers,
  1914–1945
The Russian Convoys, 1941–
  1945
The US Navy in World War
  Two
British Submarines in World
  War Two
British Cruisers in World War
  One
U-Boats of World War Two
Malta Convoys, 1940–1943

Uniforms
US Special Forces of World
  War Two
US Special Forces 1945 to the
  Present
The British Army in Northern
  Ireland
Israeli Defence Forces, 1948 to
  the Present
British Special Forces, 1945 to
  Present
US Army Uniforms Europe,
  1944–1945
The French Foreign Legion
Modern American Soldier
Israeli Elite Units
US Airborne Forces of World
  War Two
The Boer War
The Commandos World War
  Two to the Present
Victorian Colonial Wars

A catalogue listing these series and other Arms & Armour Press
titles is available on request from: Sales Department, Arms &
Armour Press, Artillery House, Artillery Row, London SW1P 1RT.